How to Sign Animals
with
Terry the Monkey

written and illustrated by

Joe Jacobs

for Lou, Eddie & Emily x

How to Sign Animals

with **Terry the Monkey**

1 — zoo animals

2 — pet animals

3 — farm animals

4 — sea animals

5 — garden animals

1

zoo animals

To sign **elephant**, make a full 'C' hand (by curling your fingers into a 'C') in front of your nose and move it forwards and downwards and forwards and upwards, in the shape of an elephant's trunk.

To sign **lion**, make claw shapes and move your hands down and around the sides of your head, like a lion's mane, then make clawing movements in front of your body.

To sign **camel**, make a flat hand and move it to the right and up and down in the shape of a camel's humps.

To sign **hippo**, hold one fist above the other and twist your hands apart like jaws.

To sign **giraffe**, make a full 'C' hand (by curling your fingers into a 'C') and move the hand upwards in front of your neck and face.

To sign **tiger**, flex your fingers and move your hands apart in front of your chest to make stripes then slowly make claws in front of your body, wrinkling your nose like a tiger.

To sign **kangaroo**, hold your index and middle fingers your body then make forwards jumping movements with your hands.

To sign **penguin**, hold your hands flat at your sides with palms facing downwards and make short movements from side to side.

To sign **crocodile**, make your hands into claws and hold one on top of the other. Touch your hands together twice, like a crocodile snapping its jaws.

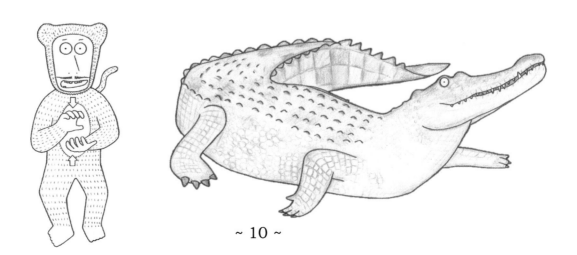

To sign **rhino**, move your hand upwards
from your nose in the shape of a rhino's horn.

To sign **zebra**, fingerspell 'Z' by touching your left palm with the tips
of your right fingers then draw stripes across your body.

To sign **panda**, make circles around your eyes
with your index fingers.

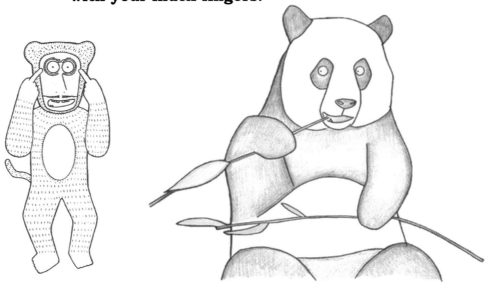

To sign **wolf**, bend your fingers and point your thumb then move your
hand away from your nose, bunching your fingers.

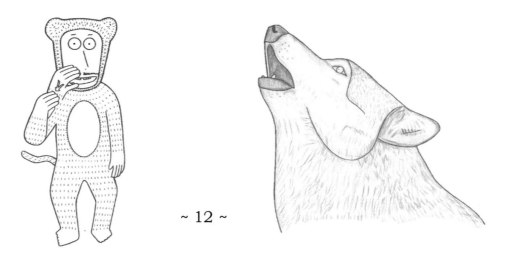

To sign **sloth**, fingerspell the letter 's', 'l', 'o', 't', 'h'.

s

l

o

t

h

To sign **monkey**, brush your sides with the backs of your hands.

To sign **gorilla**, pretend to beat your chest like a gorilla.

2

Dog

pet animals

To sign **cat**, flex your fingers and move your hands apart from the sides of your mouth.

To sign **dog**, point your index and middle fingers downwards and make two short downward movements.

To sign **rabbit**, make rabbit ears with your index and middle fingers and twitch them at the sides of your head.

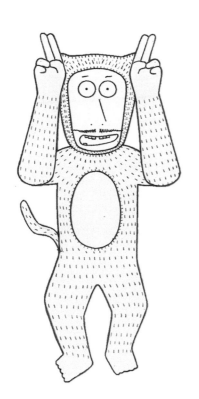

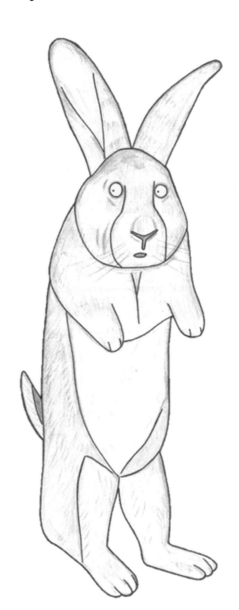

~ 17 ~

'This is how you sign "rabbit."'
'Can I keep him, Eddie?'

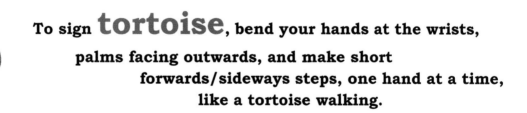

To sign **tortoise**, bend your hands at the wrists, palms facing outwards, and make short forwards/sideways steps, one hand at a time, like a tortoise walking.

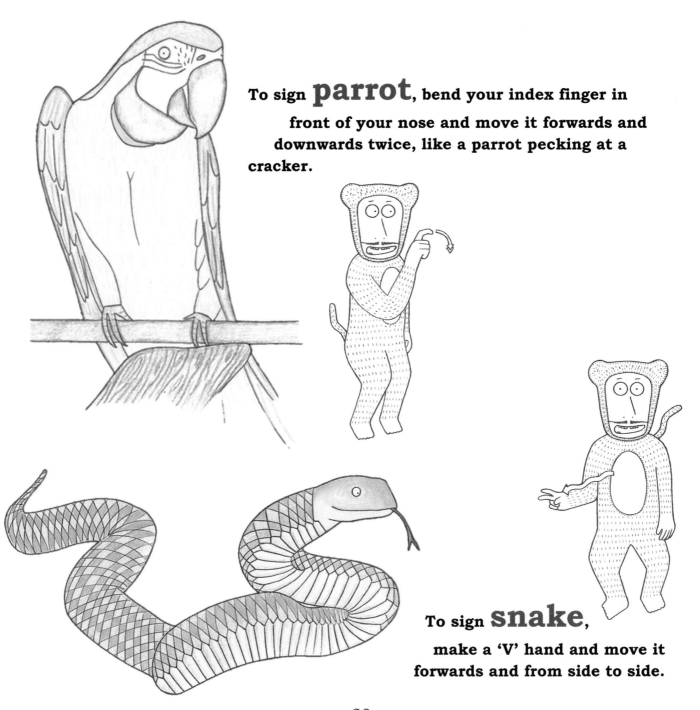

To sign **parrot**, bend your index finger in front of your nose and move it forwards and downwards twice, like a parrot pecking at a cracker.

To sign **snake**, make a 'V' hand and move it forwards and from side to side.

To sign **guinea pig**, fingerspell the letter 'g' (by placing your right fist on top of your left fist) then sign 'pig' by making tight circles in front of your nose with your fist.

g

To sign goldfish, sign 'gold' by fingerspelling 'g' and springing open your fingers, then sign 'fish' by moving your hand forwards and from side to side like a fish.

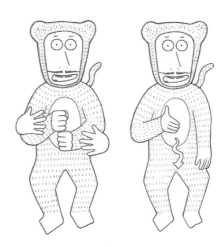

To sign **unicorn**, make a horn shape moving your hand upwards from your forehead.

To sign **dinosaur**, hunch your shoulders and make your hands into claws then move one hand at a time like a dinosaur walking.

3

farm animals

To sign pig, make a fist and move it in circles in front of your nose.

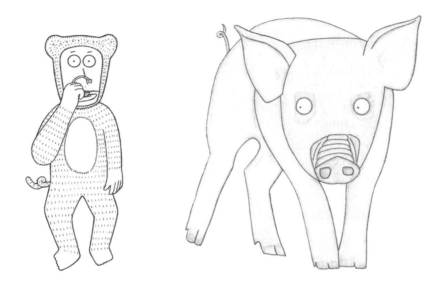

To sign chicken, stick out your elbows and flap them like wings.

To sign **turkey**, extend your thumb, index and middle fingers
and waggle them from side to side below your chin.

To sign **duck**, bend your fingers and thumb and
open and close them in front of your mouth like a duck's beak.

To sign **sheep**, stick out your little fingers and make forward circles at the sides of your head like a ram's horns.

To sign **horse**, fingerspell 'G' (by placing your right fist on top of your left fist) and move your hands up and down as though holding reins.

To sign **donkey**, hold your hands with palms facing forwards at the sides of your head and bend your fingers forwards twice.

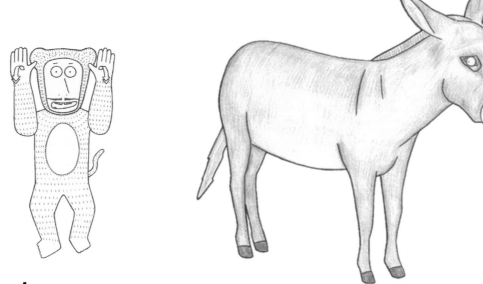

To sign **goat**, curl all your fingers into a 'C' by your chin then move your hand forwards as you close it into a fist.

To sign **COW**, make 'Y' hands (by sticking out your thumbs and little fingers) and twist them upwards at the sides of you head.

To sign **bull**, make a nose ring with your thumb and index finger.

4

sea animals

To sign **whale**, make an 'O' hand on top of your head and spring open your fingers several times, like a blowhole.

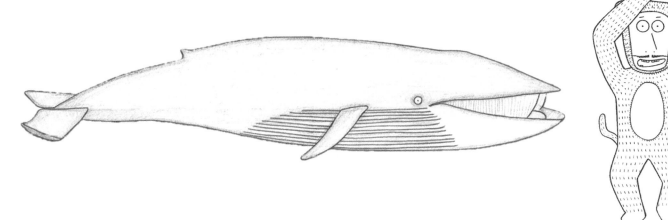

To sign **dolphin**, bend your right hand at the wrist and move your hand up and down as it moves to your left, like a leaping dolphin.

To sign **crab**, open and close the thumb and index fingers like claws as you move your hands to the left.

To sign **fish**, move a flat, upright hand forwards and from side to side like a fish swimming.

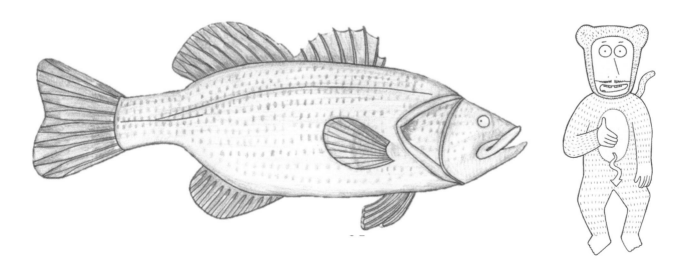

To sign **octopus**, move your hands forwards and outwards, flexing and pointing your index fingers like tentacles.

To sign **seal**, keep your hands flat and turned outwards and make circular movements while moving your shoulders up and down.

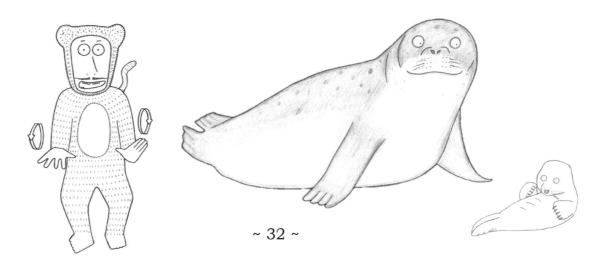

To sign **shark**, hold your right hand flat and upright in front of your chest and move it slowly forward, like a shark's fin moving through the water.

5

garden animals

To sign **squirrel**, make a full 'C' hand (by curling your fingers into a 'C') and move it upwards and outwards from the side of your body.

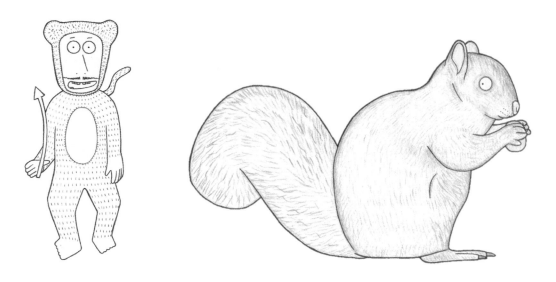

To sign **badger**, make a stripe from your nose up over your head.

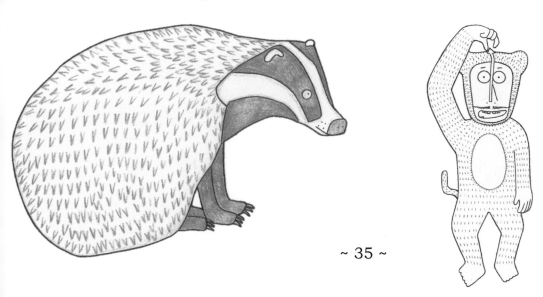

To sign **spider**, make a claw with your right hand and wiggle your fingers like spider's legs as your hand crawls up your left arm.

To sign **fly**, make an 'O' with your thumb and index finger and move it forwards in small side to side movements.

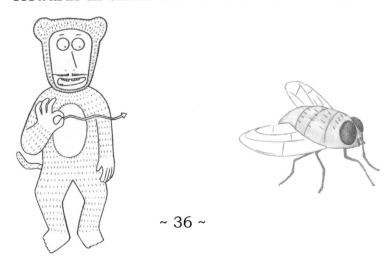

To sign **frog**, make a full 'C' hand and make short movements forwards and backwards in front of your throat like a frog breathing.

To sign **fox**, bend your hand with the fingers pointing back at your nose then bunch your fingers as you move the hand sharply forwards.

To sign **bird**, open and close your thumb and index finger in front of your mouth, like a beak.

To sign **butterfly**, cross your hands in front of your chest with your thumbs interlocked and bend your fingers from the knuckles so that your hands flap like butterfly wings.

To sign **worm**, bend and straighten your index finger as it moves to your left.

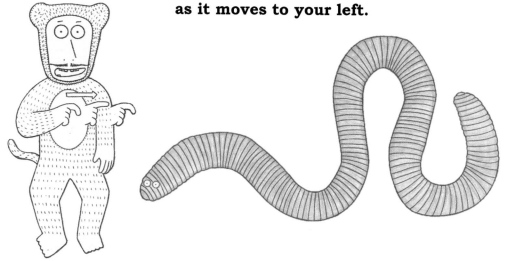

To sign **snail**, extend your index and middle fingers then make a fist with your left hand and place it on the back of your right hand like a shell and move both hands slowly forwards.

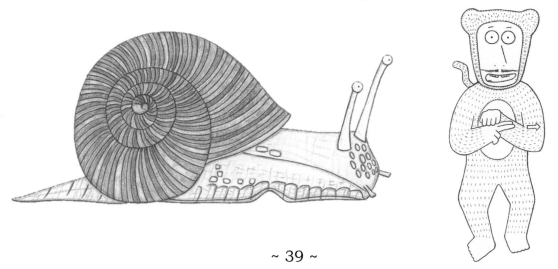

~ 39 ~

To sign **mouse**, touch the side of your nose with your index finger and twist your hand from the wrist.

To sign **bat**, make a 'V' with your right hand and bend the fingers so that they hook over the index and middle fingers of your left hand.

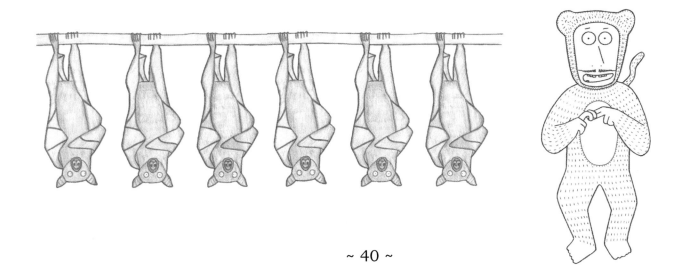

To sign peacock, make 'O' hands and hold them in front of your body then move your hands up and around while opening your fingers like a peacock's fan.

~ 41 ~

Try to mouth, or say, the words in this book as you sign them. Experienced signers focus on the mouth of the person they are signing with and follow hand movements with their peripheral vision. Signing is not a game of charades, so it is not cheating if you speak! Be animated in your facial expressions (for example, wrinkle your nose when signing tiger) as this will make your signing lively and easier to follow. Terry the Monkey is right-handed and the signs in this book show how a right-handed monkey (or human) would sign. If you are left-handed, reverse the roles of the hands. The best way to learn sign language will always be face to face with a teacher, but I hope that Terry the Monkey can make sign language fun and accessible for children. This book is intended solely for entertainment, but every care has been taken to ensure the signs are accurate and widely used and recognised.

Like you, Terry the Monkey is learning new signs every day. To find out more about sign language and the full range of Terry the Monkey books, follow Terry on Instagram (@officialterrythemonkey) or visit **terrythemonkey.com**

How to Sign Animals with Terry the Monkey is now available as an ebook and as an American Sign Language edition from Amazon. Other titles in the Terry the Monkey series include *How to Sign Food*, *How to Sign with Babies*, *How to Sign Halloween* and *How to Sign Christmas*. Joe Jacobs' books are reviewed by deaf parents and children on the National Deaf Children's Society's website (ndcs.org.uk) and in *Families* magazine. Please support the NDCS. Joe Jacobs is a regular contributor to limpingchicken.com, the world's most popular deaf blog, where you can read more about Terry the Monkey.

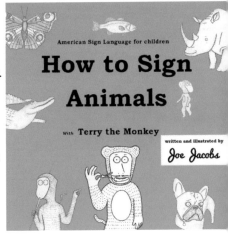

Printed in Great
Britain
by Amazon